WILD WEATHER

Science Adventures with Sonny the Origami Bird

by Thomas Kingsley Troupe

illustrated by Jamey Christoph

PICTURE WINDOW BOOKS
a capstone imprint

High up, along a mountain trail, a hiker sat and folded an origami bird.

"It sure is sunny," she said. As she held the bird high, a gust of wind lifted the paper. The bird began to fly.

"Whoa, how did it get so windy?"

Just then, the bird spotted a duck flying nearby.

2

"Hey, there. What's your name?"

The bird remembered the hiker had said *sunny*.

"Sonny, I think."

"I'm chuck. Nice to meet you, sonny. Say, I've got a real problem. My wife, Natasha, is missing. We were trying to fly away from here."

3

WARM AIR

COOL AIR

"It's simple," he said. "The sun heats the land, making the air above it warm. The warm air rises. Cool air rushes to take the place of the warm air. And because Earth spins, wind can come from any direction."

"So, do you think the wind carried Natasha away?" Sonny asked.

"I hope not," Chuck cried. "She was right next to me, but then she disappeared!"

A drop of water struck Sonny's wing.

"Just what we need! It's **raining!** Fly underneath me, sonny. I don't think wet paper is good for flying."

"**Clouds** and **rain**? How did they get here?"

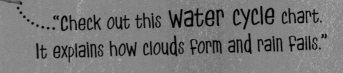

"...Check out this **water cycle** chart. It explains how clouds form and rain falls."

"WOW! That's pretty simple, really."

WATER CYCLE

The sun heats water on the ground, turning it into an invisible gas.

Gas rises, cools, and turns into water droplets.

Water droplets clump together to form clouds.

Water droplets combine and fall as rain.

"So rain is just a bunch of tiny droplets?" Sonny said. "That doesn't seem so bad."

"Normal rainstorms are fine. But thunderstorms can make lightning and heavy rain. When too much rain falls all at once, a flood can form."

"Whoa!"

"Hang on," Chuck yelled. "Hail is falling!"

"Hail?" Sonny chirped. "What's that?"

"Sometimes storm clouds called cumulonimbus clouds form. Water droplets in the highest parts of the cloud bounce around and freeze into ice pellets," Chuck said. "The pellets hit water droplets, and the hail gets bigger."

"And once the hail is too heavy, it falls?" Sonny asked.

"You got it," Chuck shouted. "Come on, let's head for the woods!"

"Weather tools?"
Sonny asked. "Like what?"

ANEMOMETER

GS 405 kts
217/66

HGD

DST 76 nm
19:48

22

23

24

25

21

0

KBKW

RADAR

60

60

40

40

SATELLITE

"They have instruments to measure wind speed and direction," Chuck explained. "And radar to track rain and thunderstorms. Meteorologists even use satellites in outer space to track how and where the clouds move."

Sonny shivered. His papery body was growing cold.

"Natasha is lost, and it will snow any day now."
Chuck quacked sadly.

"So what's the deal with snow?"

"It's a bit different than hail. The water vapor turns into an ice crystal. The ice crystal clings to other crystals and forms a snowflake."

"That doesn't sound so bad," Sonny said.

"If the ground and air are cold enough, the snowflakes pile up and cover the ground," Chuck quacked. "The lakes freeze, and it's tough for birds like us to find food."

"Oh! So that's why you **fly south!**"

"I'm not flying south without my wife! NaTasha!" Chucked quacked. "Where are you?"

"How's the weather down south?"

"It's much warmer. But the weather can get wild there too."

"What do you mean?" Sonny asked.

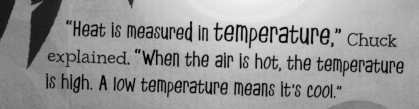

"Heat is measured in temperature," Chuck explained. "When the air is hot, the temperature is high. A low temperature means it's cool."

"That makes sense," Sonny said.

"Too much heat can hurt people, plants ... even animals," Chuck quacked. "During a heat wave, the temperature and humidity stay high for two or more days."

"I wouldn't want to be stuck in one of those!" Sonny said.

Where was the worst heat wave on record? That would be "down under." The temperature in Marble Bar, Australia, was over 100 degrees Fahrenheit (38 degrees Celsius) for 160 days in a row in 1923. Hot days, mate!

"Where is Natasha? she couldn't have just **disappeared!**"

"What happened to those trees?"

"A tornado came through here years ago," Chuck said.

"What's a **tornado?**" Sonny asked.

"It's a funnel of wind that forms in the sky and wrecks what it touches on the ground," chuck said. "Tornadoes form during a thunderstorm. They are more likely to occur over flat land."

"But how?" Sonny asked.

"When the wind in a storm changes direction, increases speed, and rises, it makes the air below it spin. Rising air pushes the spinning column of air downward until it's vertical. The spinning funnel of air speeds up, forming a tornado."

Tornadoes are usually determined to be weak, strong, or violent. The violent ones can have winds in excess of 200 miles (322 kilometers) per hour. They can destroy homes. Only 2 percent of tornadoes are violent.

"I had no idea weather could be so **scary**," Sonny said.

"That's nothing. My cousin Frank almost got caught in a **hurricane** once."

"A **hurricane**? I'm afraid to ask!"

"A hurricane forms in summer or fall," Chuck said. "It forms over an ocean and moves toward land."

"Does it make lots of wind like a tornado?" asked Sonny.

"Yes. Strong winds rotate around the 'eye' of the storm," said Chuck. "The spinning storm picks up energy from the warmth of the ocean. When it hits land, high winds and heavy rain can damage buildings."

The "eye" of a hurricane is the spot in the center of the storm. In the eye, the winds are light or calm, clouds break up and rain ends as the sky clears.

"WOW, all that dangerous weather scares me!" said Sonny.

"Here's the thing, sonny," chuck said. "we can't control weather. But meteorologists can warn everyone when dangerous weather is coming, and we can prepare for it."

"Hey, chuck. Is that your wife?"

"It is! where were you, Natasha?"

"I went back for my sunglasses. I can't fly south without them!"

"Come with us, sonny," Chuck said.

"I'd love to!" sonny said. "But can I get some of those cool sonny-glasses too?"

GLOSSARY

crystal—a solid, clear formation sometimes made of minerals or ice

cumulonimbus—a cloud that makes a thunderstorm

droplet—a small drop of water

funnel—a cone-shape with an open top and bottom; tornadoes are often shaped like funnels

instrument—a tool that gets information

meteorologist—a person who studies and predicts the weather

pellet—a small, rounded piece of material

predict—to tell something will happen before it does

radar—a weather tool that sends out microwaves to determine the size, strength, and movement of storms

rotate—to spin around

satellite—a device launched into orbit, built to circle Earth or other planets

water vapor—a gas made from a liquid

vertical—straight up and down

violent—very strong and powerful

READ MORE

Gibbons, Gail. *Tornadoes!* New York: Holiday House, 2009.

Harris, Caroline. *Weather.* Discover Science. New York: Kingfisher, 2012.

Spilsbury, Louise, and Richard Spilsbury. *Raging Floods.* Awesome Forces of Nature. Chicago: Heinemann, 2010.

MAKE AN ORIGAMI BIRD

Sonny sure learned a lot about weather! Want to make your own paper bird? Check out these instructions to make an origami dove.

what you need

origami paper

WHAT YOU DO

Folds

Valley folds are shown with a dashed line. One side of the paper is folded against the other like a book. A sharp fold is made by running your finger along the fold line.

Reverse folds are shown with an orange dashed and dotted line. They are made by opening a pocket slightly and folding the model inside itself along existing creases.

Arrows

single-pointed arrow: Fold the paper in the direction of the arrow.

double-pointed arrow: Fold the paper and then unfold it.

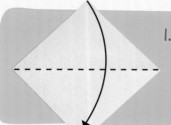

1. Start with the colored side of the paper face down. Valley fold the top corner to the bottom corner and unfold.

2. Valley fold the left corner to the right corner.

3. Valley fold the right corner's top layer to the left. Make the fold about 1.5 inches (3.8 centimeters) from the left edge.

4. Valley fold the top point to the bottom point.

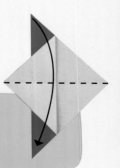

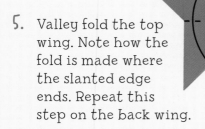

5. Valley fold the top wing. Note how the fold is made where the slanted edge ends. Repeat this step on the back wing.

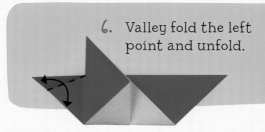

6. Valley fold the left point and unfold.

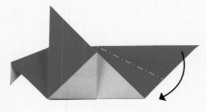

7. Inside reverse fold on the fold from step 6. This fold allows the point to swing down inside the model. When finished, a small triangle sticks out from the left side of the model.

8. Valley fold the top-right edge to the slanted edge. Make a firm fold, and unfold.

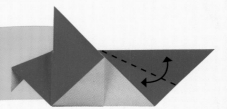

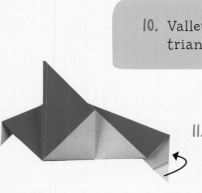

9. Inside reverse fold on the fold from step 8. This fold allows the right point to swing down inside the model. When finished, a small triangle sticks out from the right side of the model.

10. Valley fold the top of the right triangle and unfold.

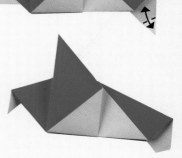

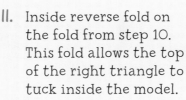

11. Inside reverse fold on the fold from step 10. This fold allows the top of the right triangle to tuck inside the model.

INDEX

INTERNET SITES

FactHound offers a safe, fun way to find Internet sites related to this book. All of the sites on FactHound have been researched by our staff.

Here's all you do:

Visit *www.facthound.com*

Type in this code: 9781479521883

more books in the series:

Diggin' Dirt: Science Adventures with Kitanai the Origami Dog

Glowing with Electricity: Science Adventures with Glenda the Origami Firefly

Lookin' for Light: Science Adventures with Manny the Origami Moth

Simply Sound: Science Adventures with Jasper the Origami Bat

Thanks to our advisers for their expertise, research, and advice:
Joseph M. Moran, PhD, Professor Emeritus
University of Wisconsin, Green Bay

Terry Flaherty, PhD, Professor of English
Minnesota State University, Mankato

Editor: Shelly Lyons
Designer: Ashlee Suker
Art Director: Nathan Gassman
Production Specialist: Eric Manske
The illustrations in this book were created digitally.

Picture Window Books are published by Capstone,
1710 Roe Crest Drive, North Mankato, Minnesota 56003
www.capstonepub.com

Library of Congress Cataloging-in-Publication Data
Troupe, Thomas Kingsley, author.
Wild weather : science adventures with Sonny the origami bird / by Thomas Kingsley Troupe.
pages cm. — (Nonfiction picture books. Origami science adventures)
Summary: "Engaging text and colorful illustrations and photos teach readers about weather"— Provided by publisher.
Audience: 4-8
Audience: Grade K to 3.
Includes bibliographical references and index.
ISBN 978-1-4795-2188-3 (library binding)
ISBN 978-1-4795-2945-2 (paperback)
ISBN 978-1-4795-3324-4 (ebook pdf)
1. Weather—Juvenile literature. 2. Birds—Juvenile literature. 3. Ducks—Juvenile literature. 4. Origami—Juvenile literature. I. Title.
QC981.3.T76 2014
551.6—dc23   2013032502

Photo credits
Digital illustrations include royalty-free images from Shutterstock.

Capstone Studio: Karon Dubke, 22-23; Shutterstock: B747, 19 (back), ChameleonsEye, 15, Ivsanmas, 11 (radar), Mechanik, 11 (satellite), razlomov, 19 (bottom), T.W. van Urk, 11 (anemometer)

Printed in the United States of America in Stevens Point, Wisconsin.
092013   007768WZS14